DK ESSENTIAL MANAGERS

Working with Difficult People

RAPHAEL LAPIN

D1022422

London, New York, Munich,
Melbourne, and Delhi

Editor Daniel Mills
US Editor Charles Wills
Senior Art Editor Helen Spencer
Production Editor Ben Marcus
Production Controller Hema Gohil
Executive Managing Editor Adèle Hayward
Managing Art Editor Kat Mead
Art Director Peter Luff
Publisher Stephanie Jackson

DK DELHI
Editor Ankush Saikia
Design Manager Arunesh Talapatra
DTP Designer Pushpak Tyagi

First American Edition, 2009

Published in the United States by DK Publishing
375 Hudson Street, New York, New York 10014

09 10 11 12 10 9 8 7 6 5 4 3 2 1

ND138—September 2009

Published in Great Britain by
Dorling Kindersley Limited.

A catalog record for this book is available from
the Library of Congress.

ISBN 978-0-7566-5253-1

DK books are available at special discounts
when purchased in bulk for sales promotions,
premiums, fund-raising, or educational use.
For details, contact: DK Publishing Special Markets,
375 Hudson Street, New York, New York 10014 or
SpecialSales@dk.com.

Color reproduction
by Colorscan, Singapore
Printed in China by WKT

Discover more at **www.dk.com**

Contents

Introduction

The skill of an effective manager is measured not only by how well they manage their motivated employees, but also by how well they work with the difficult people on their team. A difficult employee can have a negative impact on the performance of the entire group, and yet very few managers have the necessary skills to manage the difficult team member.

To harness the strengths of the difficult person and secure their cooperation, you need to develop the relevant skills, refine your technique, and apply disciplined processes. This book introduces the key techniques and skills that are essential to working with difficult people.

As you build competency, you will become capable of successfully transforming a potentially frustrating experience into a satisfying and productive one. *Working with Difficult People* provides you with the tools and processes which will allow you to effectively manage the difficult employee.

This book also touches on the reasons behind difficult behavior and how to respond to them. You will learn skills that will make you a better communicator, and this will change the way you approach conflict and allow you to forge strong working relationships. Your managerial skills will improve as you use this book to navigate the human dynamics of the workplace.

Chapter 1

Understanding difficult people

People are often difficult because you allow them to be so. If you uncover the cause for their difficult behavior, take responsibility for it, and apply steps to manage it, you can turn even the most difficult person into a productive, happy, and loyal employee.

Changing your mindset

When faced with difficult people you might throw up your hands in despair and attribute the problem to their aggravating personality. Although you can sometimes walk away, mostly you need to work with them. Realize that you can influence their behavior by vigilantly managing your own.

TIP

RESPOND THOUGHTFULLY

Try not to react impulsively when dealing with a difficult person. Think before you respond: it will advance the interaction and make the other person feel they are being taken seriously.

Focusing on behavior

While you cannot change people, you can influence their behavior. It is therefore useful to see the *behavior* as difficult rather than the *people*. When you perceive *people* to be difficult, you see yourself as a victim and allow them to hold power over you. This can make you frustrated, angry, and defensive, and cause you to react negatively. Separating the two will make it easier for you to achieve perspective. It will help you manage your emotions, be objective, and respond with thoughtfulness and purpose. This change in mindset is the first step in dealing with difficult behavior.

Using influence

When faced with difficult behavior, we tend to assert our own demands, thus generating resistance in the other person. However, we can influence their behavior by engaging and working with them rather than against them. This involves a careful application of processes, techniques, and skills that can achieve collaboration.

Taking responsibility

To manage people who show difficult behavior, you must first take responsibility for your contribution to their behavior. You may be enabling them to behave difficultly without realizing it. For example, you may be passive, thereby telling them their behavior is acceptable. Or you may react aggressively and engage them in further battle. You may talk *at* them rather than *to* them, making them defensive. It could also be a seemingly minor issue, such as your body language, tone of voice, or facial expression.

TIP

MENDING RELATIONSHIPS

If a relationship is becoming strained because of the other person's behavior, analyze what you might be doing to contribute to that behavior, and how you might change it.

TAKING CONTROL

FAST TRACK

OFF TRACK

FAST TRACK	OFF TRACK
Thinking I can alter their behavior	Thinking they will never change
Thinking maybe I am to blame too	Thinking it is all their fault
Understanding their motives	Thinking they are unreasonable
Thinking I can resolve this with them	Thinking there is nothing I can do
Refusing to be a passive victim	Getting angry and frustrated

Creating a useful framework

When you are working with difficult people, a useful framework to apply is one that is made of three fundamental components: managing the relationship, engaging the other person in dialog, and negotiating* a working solution. Each of these involves skills that, when mastered, will enhance your effectiveness as a leader.

*Negotiating — *working together to design a solution that meets the needs of all parties involved.*

Managing the relationship

By the time a person has become difficult with you in the workplace, you can assume that your relationship with them is also in distress. This can be caused by an underlying resentment, anger, mistrust, or any other relationship stressor that they feel. It is common for managers to ignore the relationship issue and attempt to address the problem at hand directly. This seldom works because a stressed relationship does not lead to constructive dialog. You cannot resolve the problem at hand without first repairing the relationship, at least to the extent that effective dialog can take place.

Engaging in dialog

A crucial component of the "working with difficult people" framework is engaging in productive dialog. When faced with a difficult person, avoid presenting them with a monolog about your demands. If one or both parties talk but neither listens, communication is ineffective and does little to advance understanding. Productive dialog expands the scope of discussion and digs out relevant information. It reveals deeper concerns without which you cannot work toward resolution. Also, as information is exchanged and understanding is achieved, dialog lays the foundation for lasting resolution.

Negotiating a working solution

The final key component in the framework is negotiating a working solution. After restoring the relationship and understanding one another's needs through dialog, you will be ready to search for a workable solution. You should strive to construct a solution that addresses everyone's needs, and involve all parties in the process by inviting them to contribute ideas. This is important as it will give them a stake in the outcome. Remain open to creative solutions, and do not be limited to preconceived ideas and old ways of doing things. Your negotiation process should be innovative and collaborative, not restrictive and threatening. This approach will help achieve amicable and durable solutions.

HOW TO...
USE THE FRAMEWORK

> Listen to the other person with sympathy and without defending your position.

> Then summarize your understanding of their position and check this with them.

> Next, inquire by asking clarifying questions to expand dialog.

> Encourage the other person to discuss their needs, and show interest in them.

> Share your needs and concerns with them in a composed and friendly way.

> Jointly explore options that could potentially satisfy both your needs.

> Be creative and open-minded when you look for solutions, and invite others' ideas.

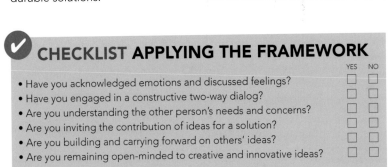

✓ CHECKLIST **APPLYING THE FRAMEWORK**

	YES	NO
• Have you acknowledged emotions and discussed feelings?	☐	☐
• Have you engaged in a constructive two-way dialog?	☐	☐
• Are you understanding the other person's needs and concerns?	☐	☐
• Are you inviting the contribution of ideas for a solution?	☐	☐
• Are you building and carrying forward on others' ideas?	☐	☐
• Are you remaining open-minded to creative and innovative ideas?	☐	☐

Building competency

Encountering difficult people in the workplace is inevitable, yet most of us do not have the competency to deal with them. It is not taught in business schools, but is an invaluable asset in the manager's repertoire. Competency results from disciplined processes, refined techniques, and strong skills.

HOW TO... UNCOVER HIDDEN FEELINGS

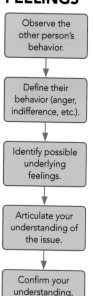

Observe the other person's behavior.

Define their behavior (anger, indifference, etc.).

Identify possible underlying feelings.

Articulate your understanding of the issue.

Confirm your understanding, but be open.

Engage them in further discussion.

Having a process

A process is a series of steps or actions that, when implemented properly, achieves a desired result. Just as a process is necessary in any complex operation, it is also essential to the success of any difficult human interaction. When facing a difficult person, you probably react impulsively, and at times confrontationally. This is because you have no roadmap to show you the way; in short, you lack a process. The more learned processes you have at your disposal, the better equipped you will be to deal with difficult behavior. An example of such a process is the six-step model (see left) for analyzing difficult behavior to uncover the underlying deeper feeelings.

Refining your technique

As you learn to implement the processes, you will find that you develop techniques of your own that sit well with you and fit your unique personality. Techniques here refer to the methods you use to best apply the steps of a process. It may be the phraseology you choose, the way you ask questions, or how you use body language to put the other person at ease. The process, however, will always provide the framework within which to apply the technique. As you learn to implement these processes* and techniques there will be a period of initial awkwardness, as with any learning. Make sure that you persevere, and within a short time you will find your competency improving. As you become more comfortable, be prepared to experiment with some of your own techniques, too, and before long they will feel very much a part of you.

*Process —
A process is a framework which provides a manageable and repeatable system to successfully accomplish a complex operation or interaction.

Developing strong skills

The final part of achieving competency is developing skills. You can strengthen your competency by extensively practicing the processes and techniques. The more you practice, the better you will get, and, in time, you will notice that you are able to deal with challenging situations with composure and grace, even while optimizing results. Use every opportunity to practice dealing with difficult behavior and strive to become a master at working with difficult people. This will enhance your managerial capacity and provide you with a competitive edge in today's challenging workplace.

HIGH LEVEL OF COMPETENCY

PRACTICED SKILL

=

REFINED TECHNIQUE

+

DISCIPLINED PROCESS

+

Addressing root causes

When dealing with a difficult person, you may be trying to deal only with their behavior, rather than uncovering the behavior's cause. This is like a doctor treating a patient's symptoms instead of the disease. To deal with difficult behavior, you must learn to uncover and articulate its root causes.

Recognizing the symptoms

The key to dealing with difficult behavior is to recognize that the behavior is a symptom that usually has an underlying emotional cause. People may get defensive (behavior) when they are unjustly blamed (cause), or get angry (behavior) when they feel unfairly treated (cause). The underlying causes need to be discussed. Once made explicit, they will lead to understanding and productive discussion. It is important to broach this topic in a non-judgmental way. This will engage the difficult person, rather than causing them to close up and become even more difficult.

INDIFFERENCE

Loss of interest or motiva[tion;]
too much work,
or too routine work;
uncomfortable with
co-workers; lack
of recognition
for previous
efforts.

Understanding the causes

When a person exhibits difficult behavior, try to understand what fear, concern, or need is driving it. Say you are in a meeting discussing a project delay and a team member angrily says "If she had sent us the information we requested on time, we would have been on schedule." This anger is driven by the team member's frustration at not receiving the requested information on time. Expose the *cause*, and not the symptom, by checking your understanding with them: "So your frustration comes from not getting the important information on time?" This will then lead to discussion of ways to streamline information flow in the future.

Root causes underlying difficult behaviors

ASSERTING BLAME

NON-COMPLIANCE

ANGER

DEFENSIVENESS

Desire for more autonomy and say; doesn't trust, understand, or agree with management; vague and unclear objectives.

Unjustly blamed; threat from co-workers; fear of tarnished image; feeling attacked.

Frustration; feeling of being exploited or unfairly treated at work; not being respected; needs not being met.

Insecure; wants to appear strong; concerned about others' perceptions; worried about career.

Transforming confrontation

Difficult people can draw you into playing their confrontational "game" without you even realizing it. When they raise their voice, you raise yours; when they assert demands, you assert counter-demands; and when they threaten you, you threaten them back. To work productively with difficult people, it is crucial that you change their game by changing your own.

TIP

RESIST ASSERTING YOUR DEMANDS

When you are confronted with demands from the other party, resist the urge to counter-demand. Instead, ask questions that will help you understand the other side's needs better.

Understanding their game

Difficult people like to engage in confrontation rather than collaboration. They try to engage you in a battle of wills with the intent of dominating you. They use tricks and intimidate you. They perceive you as an adversary rather than a co-operative problem solver, and their objective is to "win" as opposed to meeting everyone's needs. Unless you have a process of your own, you are likely to be drawn into playing the game their way. This results in distressed relationships, erosion of trust, and sub-optimal outcomes.

Changing their game

To work better with difficult people, you must change their game of war and tactics to your game of diplomacy and authenticity. Any time your interests are being threatened, it is quite normal to want to defend them. However, when you become defensive, you cause the other party to become defensive too, so that the opportunity for productive exchange is obstructed. To change the game, resist the urge to immediately defend your position. Instead, adopt an attitude of inquiry, a mindset of learning, and an open mind. Suspend your views and positions and make every effort to probe, learn, and understand the other person's views. This will advance productive dialog dramatically.

BEING COLLABORATIVE

FAST TRACK

OFF TRACK

FAST TRACK	OFF TRACK
Resisting the urge to defend	Interrupting and talking at them
Keeping an open mind	Imposing your views
Suspending your judgment	Matching their negative behavior tit-for-tat
Asking relevant questions	Becoming defensive
Maintaining an atmosphere of respect	Showing disinterest

Using collaboration

To build collaboration, you must cultivate a collaborative mindset as opposed to an adversarial one. The adversarial mindset says that if they win, you lose, while the collaborator understands that you can work out a creative solution that meets both your needs. An adversarial mindset does not trust the other party, whereas the collaborative mindset seeks ways to build trust and relationships. An adversarial mindset thinks that you have to assert your demands relentlessly, but a collaborative one tries to understand what the other party's concerns and needs are.

CASE STUDY

Altering the game plan

During negotiations with the labor union, the president of a large South African steel company demanded that the man-hours per ton be cut down. When the union representative heard this, he assumed it meant some steel workers would lose their jobs and became angry. He was on the verge of turning defensive and threatening to stage a strike if a single worker lost his job. Instead, he altered the game. He resisted the urge to defend his position and adopted an attitude of inquiry. He asked the president why he believed a cut in man-hours was necessary. The president explained his concern about their competitors' plants being more efficient. This then led to productive brainstorming for other ways to become more competitive.

Chapter 2
Communicating with excellence

Effective communication drives all successful human interaction. You can develop and refine your communication skills so that you can communicate with persuasion and influence at all times, especially when faced with difficult behavior.

Overcoming barriers

To become an effective communicator, you first need to know about communication barriers and ways to avoid them. Overcoming these barriers requires the ability to negotiate cultural differences, an environment suitable for interaction, and an appreciation of the other person's viewpoint.

TIP

RESPECT OTHER CULTURES

If you do or say something that causes offense in another culture, point out politely that it was in no way intentional, but rather due to your lack of familiarity with their culture.

Understanding differences

Ambiguous communication or misunderstandings can crop up in today's globalized world where intercultural workforces are common. To prevent this, if something sounds ambiguous or makes little sense be prepared to ask questions and clarify. When dealing with other nationalities, explain to them that misunderstandings are possible due to cultural differences and invite them to question anything that does not make sense or is not clear. Although this may not eliminate misunderstandings altogether, it will go a long way toward minimizing them.

Preventing distractions

Sometimes two people may appear to be talking to one another when they are, in fact, not. Take, for example, a union representative negotiating with management in the presence of the media. The representative may be more interested in impressing their rank and file than communicating effectively with management. If you need to confer with a person you know can be difficult, create a secure environment: a time and place without distractions that could inhibit both of you from having an honest and productive discussion.

Acknowledging perceptions

An interaction is unlikely to be productive unless each side makes an effort to understand the other side's viewpoint. Try to understand how they see the situation even though you may disagree with them. Listen carefully, ask clarifying questions, and put yourself into their shoes. Acknowledge and articulate the different perceptions without trying to convince each other which is right. This will allow the other party to feel heard and understood, and advance productive communication.

CASE STUDY

Creating a safe environment
When US President Ronald Reagan met Soviet leader Mikhail Gorbachev for the 1986 Reykjavik Summit on ballistic missiles in Iceland, he stipulated that only essential personnel, such as interpreters and national security advisors, would be present, and the media would not attend. Reagan understood the importance of creating a secure environment. By doing so he was able to conduct open and honest talks, and this also led to a close and productive friendship between the two leaders.

Listening in both directions

Listening lies at the heart of effective communication, especially when dealing with difficult people. Remember that listening works in two ways: being a good listener, and being effectively listened to. Attentive listening is a competency made up of three skills: paraphrasing, clarifying, and observing. To get listened to, you can use a similar three-step process.

TIP

LISTEN, THEN SHARE YOUR THOUGHTS

People will be much more likely to listen to you when they feel you have paid attention to them.

Paraphrasing

In a meaningful exchange, you need to understand the other party, and they need to know that you have understood them. Paraphrasing what you have understood helps you check with them for accuracy. Suppose your colleague is complaining about team members not delivering assignments on time and how this is delaying a project. To paraphrase you might say: "So when assignments are not delivered on time, you become concerned about delaying the project and disappointing our customers. Is that correct?". Here you are allowing them to clarify misunderstandings, and, more importantly, you are letting them know that they have been understood.

✔ CHECKLIST **LISTENING WITH ATTENTIVENESS**

	YES	NO
• Am I listening carefully to what the other party is saying?	☐	☐
• Am I checking my understanding by summarizing and paraphrasing?	☐	☐
• Am I asking clarifying questions to discover missing information?	☐	☐
• Am I sure our communication is purposeful and productive?	☐	☐
• Am I observing their non-verbal cues and matching those with their verbal messages?	☐	☐
• Am I listening more than I am talking?	☐	☐

Clarifying

Use clarifying questions to keep the interaction focused. Often while communicating it may seem that information is missing. People may say they feel overwhelmed but not explain why, or that they feel unfairly treated but not provide a reason. Clarifying questions can uncover missing information. Suppose an employee says: "She always makes me angry," then your clarifying question could be: "When did she make you angry, and what did she do that upset you?". This expands the discussion, bringing to it a new context.

Observing

Listening attentively also includes observing non-verbal cues such as body language, voice intonation, and facial expressions. Look out for any inconsistencies between what is being said and the non-verbal cues. If you spot something like this you should point it out in a non-judgmental way. Observing non-verbal cues and matching them with verbal cues will greatly advance your ability to work with difficult people.

summarize

body language clarify

observe understand

converse intonation

listen uncover

TIP

OFFER IDEAS
Always offer your
ideas, never impose
them. People do not
like to have things
imposed upon
them and they
will often resist.

Demonstrating understanding

To be listened to, show you understand the other person.
Suppose development and marketing are discussing a
new accounting software. Development believes it will
capture the financial data business and boost revenues.
But marketing think its features and price are more
than companies would need or pay for. You could then
paraphrase: "Development sees great potential in terms
of our bottom-line, but marketing are concerned it is too
much for our typical user. Is that correct?". Both sides
will feel understood and stop asserting their positions.

Offering your idea

When both development and marketing know you
have understood them, they will be more receptive
to your ideas. Do not impose your ideas, rather offer
them. You may say: "Having understood the concerns
of both sides, one option is to design a base system
with add-on features for specific customers." When
offering your idea, bring it full circle by explaining how
it addresses the concerns of both parties. You should
also acknowledge that by expressing their concerns,
both sides have helped generate a potential solution.

validate   address

collaborate

exchange   focus

consider

question   offer

uncover

Asking questions

After offering your idea, engage both sides in further discussion and invite them to refine it and offer ideas of their own. An effective way to do this is by asking focused questions. For example: "What concerns might not be addressed by this idea, or are there any new concerns that it raises?", "What variations could further develop this idea?", or "Can you think of ideas we haven't yet considered?". By doing this you are turning potential confrontation into collaboration, generating more creative thinking, and involving both sides in the solution. When you are fluent in this three-step process and use it in your repertoire, you will find it easier to get your ideas heard and accepted.

HOW TO...
GET LISTENED TO

Show the other side you have understood them by paraphrasing them.

↓

Once they are receptive, offer your own ideas; never impose your idea.

↓

Explain how your idea addresses their concerns and needs too.

↓

Close the discussion with a focused question that engages them further.

LISTENING EFFECTIVELY

FAST TRACK

Assuming the other side has a legitimate perspective of their own
Putting genuine effort into understanding them
Making sure you listen in order to be listened to

OFF TRACK

Insisting you are right and know all the answers
Interrupting, contradicting, and trying to enforce your will
Disparaging the other side or their ideas in any way

Avoiding confrontation

Sometimes a colleague consistently fails to do what is required of them. This can be frustrating and cost the company significantly. Blaming the person is not the way to fix this. You need to avoid confronting the person and instead apply the Action, Feeling, Impact, and Request (AFIR) model.

ALWAYS USE THE AFIR MODEL

Always use the AFIR model to reframe blame even if the other party really is at fault. You will get a lot further in engaging them in problem-solving because they will not feel the need to defend themselves.

Reframing the problem

When dealing with a difficult colleague it is crucial that you choose a process which encourages dialog and joint problem-solving. You can do this by reframing the problem. Suppose a co-worker is not returning your phone calls. You could either blame him by saying: "He never returns my phone calls", or you could reframe the problem: "When my calls are not returned I feel anxious as I am unable to get the information I need." Instead of looking to blame someone, focus on what is happening, the impact it has, and what is actually needed.

Preparing the message

To prepare a non-confrontational message you need to ask the AFIR questions: what is happening? (Action), how do I feel about it? (Feeling), what impact is this having? (Impact), and, what would I like? (Request). For example, a co-worker comes in late and leaves early, disrupting everyone's schedule. You decide to confront them. First ask yourself the four questions: What is happening? (Your co-worker does not respect office timings.) How do you feel about it? (You feel exploited.) What impact is this having? (You have to pick up the slack.) What would you like? (You would like the workload to be shared fairly.) By breaking the message into AFIR steps, you have moved from assigning blame to a more productive view of the problem and its solution.

Transmitting the message

To reframe the message, put the four elements in this format: "When... (put in action), I feel... (put in feeling) because... (put in impact). Would you be willing to... (put in request)?" For example: "When you are absent from work (Action), I feel exploited (Feeling) because I have to pick up the slack (Impact). Could we find a way to deal with this (Request)?" This formula avoids putting the other party on the defensive, leaving the door open for further dialog.

TIP

PRACTICE!
These are skills like any other so practice, practice, and practice!

AVOIDING BLAME STATEMENTS USING AFIR

BLAMING STATEMENT	(A) ACTION, (F) FEELING, (I) IMPACT, (R) REQUEST	AFIR (STATEMENT AND QUESTIONS)
You are never available when needed.	**A.** Not being available. **F.** Frustrated. **I.** I cannot get feedback on the project. **R.** Regular feedback on the project.	When you are unavailable I feel frustrated because I cannot get the feedback I need. Would you be willing to talk about a set time that we could meet once a week?
You are always late with your reports.	**A.** Not receiving reports on time. **F.** Concern. **I.** Delays and customer disappointment. **R.** Receiving reports on time.	When we do not get the reports on time, I get concerned because it causes delays and ultimately customer disappointment. Would you be willing to talk about ways in which we might streamline this?
You are always interrupting me.	**A.** Not being able to express my thoughts. **F.** Frustration. **I.** Not getting a fair hearing. **R.** Listening to each other adequately.	When I am unable to finish my thoughts, I get frustrated because I am not getting a fair hearing. Could we agree to listen to each other first without interrupting and then allowing for rebuttals?
You are spending too much time on just one thing.	**A.** A lot of time being spent. **F.** Anxious. **I.** More important things may not get done. **R.** Focus on the more important things.	When I see so much time being spent on this I become anxious about whether the other important things will be achieved. Would you be willing to prioritize with me what needs to get done?

Building trust

In any working relationship, trust is essential. When you are working with difficult people, it is most likely that trust has already been impaired, and the relationship has to be rebuilt. Trust is achieved not only by *what* we communicate but also by *how* we communicate it.

Communicating with authenticity

To build trust, your communication should be authentic at all times. Be genuinely interested in what the other person is saying and listen attentively. When you speak, make sure that you are clear and purposeful, and that you say what you mean. Avoid vague and ambiguous language. Ask questions to understand better, and not just to challenge. When engaged in an interaction, ask yourself if you are communicating with authenticity. This will make you understand what might be missing and allow you to make the necessary adjustments.

Being consistent

Another aspect of building trust through communication is ensuring that your non-verbal cues are consistent with your verbal ones. Imagine telling someone you are interested in what they have to say, and then checking your e-mail when they are talking to you. This sends out an inconsistent message and undermines trust. When you engage with another person make sure your non-verbal cues send the right message. Lean forward and make eye contact. Show them you care with your body language and tone of voice. Being consistent means that your actions and your words must be consistent over time.

Taking concerns seriously

When you are working with difficult people, their perception will most likely be that you are trying to impose your interests at the expense of theirs. They will feel threatened and will not trust you. To build trust you need to change that perception. In order to achieve this you need to set a positive tone. You have to indicate that the other person's concerns are important to you, and that you wish to work to protect not just your interests but theirs too. You could say, for example, to someone who feels threatened by you: "We have had our differences, perhaps, but this relationship is important to me. I would like to reconcile our interests and to do that I would really like to know more about what you truly care about." By saying so you have set a positive tone and started to change the other person's untrusting perception.

TIP

UNDERSTAND INTERESTS AND CONCERNS

The more you learn about other people, the better equipped you will be to create specific solutions that address their concerns.

USING AUTHENTIC COMMUNICATION

NON–AUTHENTIC COMMUNICATION	WHAT YOU REALLY MEAN	AUTHENTIC COMMUNICATION
Don't you think you should talk to your boss?	I think you should talk to your boss.	What do you think you should do about your boss?
You certainly are quiet.	You are too quiet and it bothers me.	I notice that you seem quiet—is my observation correct and if so would you be willing to share with me why?
You should expect me back by noon.	I cannot make a promise to you and will not commit.	My hope is to be back by noon but I really cannot promise you. Would you like me to call you if I am running behind schedule?
I guess she is ok.	I am not sure about her.	She seems ok overall, although I have some reservations.

Using questions skillfully

Strong questioning skills are crucial to effective communication. They are used to advance dialog, focus debate, obtain information, and redirect discussion. To master questioning techniques you need to be familiar with different kinds of questions and when to use them.

Asking open-ended questions

An open-ended question is one to which there is no yes-or-no, one-word answer, but which provokes a thoughtful response. It usually engages the other party to actively participate, expands the scope of discussion, and encourages further dialog. Words that commonly introduce an open-ended question are: "what", "how", and "why". As in: "What led you to that conclusion?", "How will you implement that plan?", and "Why do you feel unfairly treated?" They are used when there is a need to uncover missing information. They also help in keeeping the discussion focused.

Asking closed-ended questions

A closed-ended question is one with a yes-or-no or other short answer. The closed-ended question limits further discussion. Examples of such questions are: "Did you tell him?" (allows only a yes-or-no answer). "When did this happen?" (has a limited day, date, and time answer). "Who did it?" or "Where did they go?" are other examples. Closed-ended questions are useful to interrupt a person who is rambling and to obtain specific information. Suppose an irate customer is complaining about the lack of service he has received from your company. A closed-ended question you can ask him is: "Have you spoken to the manager yet?" This limits him to a yes/no answer and allows you to take control.

Avoiding loaded questions

We sometimes use questions as a means to lead the other person to what we want them to do or say. These are statements, accusations, or advice disguised in the form of loaded questions. An example would be: "What did you expect?". The intent here is not inquiry but rather a statement: "How incompetent of you not to realize this." Loaded questions with agendas will make the other person defensive and obstruct communication. When using questions to advance dialog, ask them with true curiosity and a desire to understand.

ASKING YOURSELF FIRST

Before asking a question, ask yourself: "Is this a true question of inquiry or a loaded question with an agenda?".

WHEN TO USE OPEN-ENDED QUESTIONS:
- To clarify missing information
- To keep the discussion focused
- To achieve a deeper level of understanding
- To help the other side clarify their own thoughts, concerns, and interests
- To expand the scope of discussion

WHEN TO USE CLOSED-ENDED QUESTIONS:
- To get answers to very specific questions
- To interrupt a person who is in endless monolog, in order to regain control of the conversation

WHEN TO USE LOADED QUESTIONS:
- Never. They have no purpose in effective communication

Tackling negative emotions

When strong negative emotions are present, you might tend to ignore them and hope that they will just go away. But when someone is angry or upset, you cannot have productive discussions. You need to deal first with the emotions and then guide the conversation back to the substantive issues.

Responding to emotions

Suppose you are meeting with a difficult colleague to discuss their repeated tardiness. They respond with an emotional outburst, and complain how they are always picked on unfairly. Before you can resolve the tardiness issue, you must address their emotions. Acknowledge the way they feel and show them that you understand (even though you may not agree). Allow them to let off some steam, then follow up with a clarifying question. Once the emotional level has diminished, lead them back to the issue at hand.

ACKNOWLEDGING
Acknowledge their feelings, and show them you understand. ("When you were passed over for a promotion you felt you deserved, you were hurt ... correct?")

Controlling your emotions

When you lose control of your emotions, you may say things you regret later, and also risk losing your credibility. Conduct yourself with grace and composure with your colleagues. If you feel overwhelmed at times, it is crucial you control your emotions. A useful technique is to mentally detach yourself from the situation and become an objective observer. A small degree of mental detachment can go a long way in regaining control over your emotions. Another technique is silence. Resist the urge to respond immediately, and sit silently for a while to regain your composure.

TIP

MONITOR YOUR OWN EMOTIONS
Ask yourself periodically: "How am I feeling?", and "What is the emotional temperature in the room?". This awareness will help you to better control your emotions.

Ways to manage others' emotions

MONITORING
Watch for cues that their emotions have calmed, before continuing discussions on the substantive issues. Cues include body language and tone of voice.

LISTENING
Listen actively while allowing them to let off steam, and do not interrupt or defend your position. They need to express themselves before emotions can subside.

LEADING
Guide them back to the substantive issues after dealing with their emotions. ("I respect how you feel. But we need to discuss the matter, now or at a later date.")

ASKING
Ask clarifying questions to show your engagement, and to generate dialog.

Avoiding e-mail conflict

Most communication today takes place through e-mail. It is fast and efficient, but it also creates opportunities for misunderstandings to crop up. You can avoid them by making sure that your mails are accurate and convey the right "mood," and aren't written on the spur of the moment.

TIP

AVOID CAPITALS
Resist the temptation to use capital letters in e-mails (except where required by grammatical rules). They are the e-mail equivalent of shouting.

Steering clear of vagueness

Since most people at the workplace are overloaded with e-mails, it is important your message stands out by being accurate and concise. It must be simple and easy to understand. Do not put your thoughts in one long unstructured paragraph. Sort out your ideas and put them into a logical order in short paragraphs or bullet points. Avoid vague comments which can cause confusion, particularly where multiple issues are being discussed. Instead, write to the point, as in: "I agree that we meet every Wednesday at noon to discuss progress." When you receive an e-mail that is confusing, reply at once and ask for clarification. Be specific about your point of confusion, such as: "Is the scheduled meeting intended for all team members or just project leads?", rather than "Who did you mean?".

? ASK YOURSELF...
BEFORE SENDING AN E-MAIL

- Is it clear and concise?
- Does it convey the tone I wish to communicate?
- Is it professional?
- Have I put across all my points?
- Have I replied to all the queries?

Conveying the right mood

Studies have shown that in face-to-face communication almost 65 percent of your message is communicated non-verbally. This means through your tone, pitch, volume of voice, and body language. In e-mail, with no visual or auditory communication, as much as 65 percent of your message could be missed. Messages may be misinterpreted as being terse, irate, sarcastic, or impatient due to the absence of visual cues. When writing an e-mail, consider the tone you wish to convey and then read through your mail before you send it to see if it conveys what you mean.

TIP

BEING PRE-EMPTIVE

Any time a misunderstanding seems to be developing via e-mail, pick up the phone and call the other person.

Establishing e-mail guidelines

Using e-mail in complex issues that require face-to-face conversation can create serious conflict and emotional responses. Establish a set of guidelines for e-mail usage, for instance: if an e-mail is very lengthy it should not be sent, rather an agenda should be sent and a phone call scheduled; e-mail should be used only for sharing data and information or to schedule live conversations; anything of an emotional nature should be discussed over the phone or in person. Such an e-mail protocol will contribute to a more productive work environment.

IN FOCUS... APPLYING THE 24-HOUR RULE

The 24-hour rule means waiting 24 hours before sending an e-mail written in a moment of emotion, so that your response is driven by reason alone. High pressure at work can cause you to become stressed. You might want to send an angry e-mail, but this can hurt feelings and raise legal issues. You could write a mail to calm your feelings, but wait a whole day to send it. By then you will have calmed down and be able to write a more constructive e-mail.

Chapter 3

Negotiating conflict

The key to creating successful working relationships is the ability to deal with differences. Imposing your will seldom produces results. Knowing how to negotiate effectively will help you cultivate strong working relationships, even with difficult workers.

Negotiating true needs

If you are negotiating with a difficult person, do not use your authority to make demands, as this will result in low-quality work and diminished morale. Instead, try to uncover your employees' true or personal needs, and then present yours. This will lead to real collaboration and solutions.

*Position —
Your initial presenting demand, or what you want, as in: "You must be available when I need you!".

*True need —
Why you want it, the need, concern, or fear driving the position, as in: "When I need information you have access to, I would like to be able to get it in a timely manner."

Avoiding positions

When faced with a position*, do not counter with your own position. Rather, find out why that position is important to the other side and what needs of theirs would be met were that position accepted. This helps uncover their true needs*, as opposed to their negotiating positions. Many people negotiate by asserting demands or positions. Consider a manager who says to an employee: "I insist that you hand me that report by 5 p.m.", and the employee retorts with: "That's impossible!". Both sides have dug in their heels, leading to impasse and limited solution options.

Uncovering true needs

You can only reach effective solutions when true needs have been addressed. Say a union representative demands higher wages for his membership. He has presented a position, but not a true need. A good negotiator will not counter the union's position, but try to uncover its members' true needs. He might discover that they would like to pay for the occasional vacation or save for a child's college fund. So their true need is more disposable income, and not necessarily higher wages. With this new understanding in mind, an alternative option could be restructuring the healthcare plan to lower membership contributions, thereby increasing disposable income without increasing wages. Some questions to ask when uncovering true needs are:

- Why is that important to you?
- In what way would that help you?
- What concerns do you have?
- What needs of yours would be met if we did that?
- What needs of yours would not be met if we did not do that?

TIP

HELPING THE OTHER PERSON

Sometimes the other person will not have a clear sense of what their true needs are. You will then need to gently question them to draw out what is really important to them.

Sharing true needs

After uncovering and understanding the other side's true needs, you are now ready to share yours. Share your true needs as opposed to your positions, because the other side will perceive a position as a demand. Suppose a co-worker likes the window open, which is causing a draft to blow your papers off your desk. Instead of telling the person to close the window (your position), it would be less threatening and more productive to share your true need: "I am concerned about my papers blowing off my desk." You have not imposed a solution but defined the problem: how can the papers be stopped from blowing off the desk? This will then open the door to problem-solving.

TIP

PUT THE OTHER PERSON'S NEEDS FIRST

Uncover the other person's true needs before you share yours with them. They will be much more receptive once they feel understood.

Being aware of personal needs

At the workplace, you must consider both the professional and personal needs of employees. Their professional needs will relate to their job: skilled co-workers, a high-performing team, good management, or a manageable workload. They will be forthcoming about these issues. Below the surface lie personal needs, such as job security, career advancement, and recognition. These personal issues often lie at the core of problems, and are crucial in resolving conflicts.

Using self-disclosure

*Self-disclosure — *Exposing a vulnerability of your own to the other party as a means to make it comfortable and safe for them to talk about their needs and concerns.*

Self-disclosure* is a useful technique for uncovering employees' personal needs. If you suspect they feel unrecognized for their work, which is a personal need, you could make them feel comfortable by saying: "Part of my satisfaction comes from my work being recognized by my colleagues. Is this a concern with you too?". By telling them that this is important to you as well, you have created a safe environment for them to talk about their personal needs.

Discussing personal needs

An employee's hidden personal concerns are more important than the obvious ones. Employees are usually reluctant to talk about these issues, which makes them difficult to address. But they do exist, so listen carefully for clues that may help you uncover them. After uncovering personal needs it is important to generate further dialog around them to gather as much information as possible. Useful questions to ask would be in the following vein: "Tell me more about the events that caused you to feel unrecognized," or "What was it specifically that made you feel unfairly treated?", or "Describe how you would like things to be." These kinds of questions will bring relevant information to the surface that can help you deal with the problem. Often you will notice that, as constructive dialog occurs and these issues are brought to the surface, your employees will find solutions themselves while you do nothing more than listen.

TIP

RECOGNIZE THE IMPORTANCE OF PERSONAL NEEDS

When all efforts at resolving an issue have been unsuccessful, consider whether there are personal needs which remain unresolved and attempt to address them.

UNCOVERING PERSONAL NEEDS

FAST TRACK

OFF TRACK

FAST TRACK	OFF TRACK
Recognizing that there are personal needs beyond work-related issues that may not be surfacing	Working to resolve work-related issues while neglecting personal needs
Listening between the lines for clues to the personal needs of emplyees	Implying that the work environment is no place to air personal issues
Using the self-disclosure technique to create a safe place to talk about personal needs	Jumping to conclusions as to what the real issues are without really trying to listen and understand

Using collaboration

Working with difficult people will frequently give rise to conflict situations. When you are working on resolving a conflict, involve the other party in designing the solution. This will give them ownership of the agreement, making them more committed and more likely to comply with it.

*Bridging question — The key question that defines the problem by bridging both sets of needs. For example: "What ideas can we think of that will satisfy both your needs and ours at the same time?"

Defining the problem

You cannot negotiate conflict until you have a clear definition of the problem you wish to solve. To define the problem you need to communicate all the needs that must be satisfied in order for both parties to agree. Before attempting to find a solution, take time to explore the other party's needs, and then communicate yours. It is a good idea to put these needs up on a whiteboard in two columns. This will help objectify the problem and separate it from personalities. Use the "bridging question"* to define the problem This will allow you to focus on finding a mutually acceptable solution.

Brainstorming creative options

Evaluating the options

Brainstorming is a way of listing potential solutions. Invite the other person to join you as this will engage them in the process of designing the solution. Encourage creative ideas, and assure them that all ideas are welcome no matter how unrealistic, because even unworkable ideas can help to trigger more realistic ones. Capture the ideas on the white board in full view. Some ground rules for brainstorming are:
• Separate coming up with options from deciding upon solutions.
• Do not allow judgment or criticism, just generate ideas.
• Welcome all ideas.
• Do not commit to any ideas that are suggested.
• Record ideas in full view.

After you have generated and captured a good list of options, you can begin to evaluate them. You can jointly identify which of the options you both agree have potential and are willing to discuss further. These options can then be cultivated, developed, and refined as you work toward an agreement that both of you can feel satisfied with. By using this method for collaborative problem-solving you greatly enhance the chances of reaching an optimal and mutually agreeable solution. In addition, this method also allows the commitment to build incrementally so that neither party feels that they are being rushed or pressured into commitment.

✔ CHECKLIST **SOLVING PROBLEMS**

	YES	NO
• Are you using questions to understand the other party's needs?	☐	☐
• Are you checking your understanding of their needs with them?	☐	☐
• Have you asserted your needs in a friendly and composed way?	☐	☐
• Have you used the "bridging question" to define the problem?	☐	☐
• Are you engaging them in brainstorming for mutual solutions?	☐	☐
• Have you generated a range of options?	☐	☐
• Have you reached consensus on the most promising options?	☐	☐
• Have you formalized an agreement?	☐	☐

When parties in conflict dig in their heels over their demands, impasse can develop rapidly. It takes skill, patience, and persistence to guide the negotiation back toward resolution while maintaining the relationship. Reframing and questioning are good tools to break impasse.

Reframing

Impasse is reached when people are inflexible. If someone presents a rigid position to you, do not counter with an equally rigid position, but reframe the position in question. For example, a customer might say: "We do not trust you to deliver the product on time." Respond with the reframing technique by saying: "So you like the product and terms, but would like assurance of timely delivery?". You have translated their rigid declaration into a flexible statement of need, and averted potential impasse.

PARTIES TALKING AT ONE ANOTHER
Listen attentively to the other party; summarize their position before presenting your thoughts

Questioning

Impasse can also be reached when solutions are proposed too early. The more information you obtain about the other side's concerns and needs, the better equipped you are to offer solutions. Question and probe to loosen their positions and understand their needs and concerns better. If, for example, they say the slides will not be ready on time for the meeting, rather than insisting, ask (non-threatening) questions such as: "What is preventing you from having them ready on time?". By getting more information you can think of possible solutions, and steer clear of impasse.

HOW TO...
REFRAME

Listen to the other party's position.

↓

Ask yourself what their needs and concerns are.

↓

Translate them into more flexible need statements.

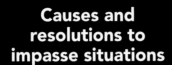

Causes and resolutions to impasse situations

RIGID POSITIONS ON BOTH SIDES
Reframe and translate rigid positions into more general and flexible statements of need.

SOLUTIONS PUT FORWARD TOO EARLY AND REJECTED
Question the other party and probe to obtain further information about their concerns and needs.

OPTIONS NOT SUFFICIENTLY EXPLORED OR EXHAUSTED
Look to change strength and/or scope of a proposal so that other options are opened up to you.

Getting past resistance

Occasionally, you might be faced with a stubborn person who refuses to engage in negotiation or problem-solving. Before throwing up your hands in utter frustration, remember that there are skills and techniques you can use to get past the resistance and guide the negotiation forward productively.

Understanding resistance

When someone refuses to engage, consider it an expression of a concern they have. You need to uncover that concern and address it appropriately. Instead of trying to engage the person in the issue at hand, talk about why they do not wish to engage. You might ask them: "What is the worst outcome that could happen if we discussed this?". They might say they are concerned about being pressured into a commitment they regret. Having understood their concerns, you could suggest an initial meeting with no expectations of commitment, thereby alleviating their fears.

Having alternatives

Before negotiating, it is crucial you consider your alternatives. What would be the best option in case the other person refuses to engage? It may be getting HR to send a warning to the individual about his performance. This can be used as leverage if absolutely necessary. For example, you could say: "I am hoping we come to an understanding because it wouldn't be good for either of us if this were to escalate further—so how should we proceed?". The purpose of alternatives is to steer the discussion back toward negotiation.

Responding to threats

Think carefully too about ways in which the other person might try to threaten you. Then consider how you can make it harder for them to do so, or ways to persuade them that such an action would be unwise. You should do this before you start to negotiate. Let's say that they try to intimidate you by threatening to tell your manager about your ineffective management skills. You could make it harder for them to pursue by briefing your manager beforehand. Then when they make their threat, you can calmly and gracefully tell them that although they are welcome to do so, you have already briefed your manager, who is fully aware of the situation. By doing this you have neutralized the threat from the difficult person, and they can no longer hold you hostage. A little thought and preparation beforehand can make a big difference later.

? **ASK YOURSELF... BEFORE ENTERING A NEGOTIATION**

- What could I do independently of the other person in the event that they are unwilling to engage?
- How can I use that as leverage to engage them?
- How might they try to threaten and intimidate me?
- What can I do or say to neutralize their threat?

CASE STUDY

Dealing with threats

The pilots' union of a major supply chain company was not pleased with how they were being compensated by management. They attempted to engage management to discuss this on several occasions, but were met each time with resistance, defiance, and refusal. Management knew that the union was in no position financially to stage a strike and therefore felt they had the upper hand. The union considered all alternatives carefully, and then decided to strengthen their option of a strike by securing a line of credit from the bank. Armed with this very real and serious alternative they approached management again and suggested that perhaps they should sit down and talk before matters escalated to a costly strike. This time around management sat down to discuss things with the union and together they were able to resolve the issues and reach an agreement.

Defusing turf wars

It is not uncommon for internal competition to exist within the organization, either between individuals or between teams. These struggles could revolve around resources, funding, project ownership, recognition, and visibility. When people are concerned about protecting their turf, this leads to performance, productivity, and morale being undermined.

Diagnosing turf wars

When teams exhibit diminished performance and productivity, one possible cause is internal competition, either within the team or between teams. Talk to the team or individuals and listen very carefully for clues that turf wars are the problem. These can be destructive if ignored, but a source of creative collaboration when resolved. Consider two competing product teams in a large corporation. Each team believes that the product on which it is working will be a key product for the company and will boost revenue and market share. Each is therefore convinced that they should have priority with regards to budget and resources. As a result each team expends enormous effort to achieve visibility for their project as they vie for the limited funds and resources. This misdirected energy causes the teams to miss deadlines, delay deliverables, and use resources inefficiently, leading ultimately to customers being left disappointed.

Reviewing objectives

The first step in resolving turf wars is facilitating dialog between the relevant teams or individuals. Each must have an understanding of their own objectives, and be able to share it. As the dialog evolves, record the objectives of each party in full view. This allows each side to absorb what the other's concerns are. It is important to encourage them to discuss not only business objectives such as revenues and growth, but personal concerns such as recognition and career advances too. Besides being an important step in resolving internal competition, this process will also help build trust and collaboration.

Aligning objectives

When dialog takes place, both sides should look for ways to align objectives so as to maximize resources and optimize efficiency. They could integrate their products and add value for customers, or collaborate on features common to both products. They could jointly market both products. They could even negotiate for both sides to achieve more visibility for their work, rather than competing for attention. Once the teams or individuals have reached an agreement, it is good practice to document the points of agreement into a charter of collaboration, to act as a roadmap for the future.

FOSTERING COOPERATION

FAST TRACK

OFF TRACK

FAST TRACK	OFF TRACK
Creating an environment that rewards collaboration	Deliberately undermining others for the purpose of competing
Engaging other teams or individuals in communication and dialog	Reacting to competitive tactics used by other people
Looking for creative ways of working together	Tolerating destructive internal competition
Taking the initiative to lead the other team into collaboration	Trying to control others rather than collaborating

Managing the agreement

You might assume that once an acceptable resolution has been reached, the negotiation is complete. This might be true where there is no ongoing working relationship. In the average work environment, however, you usually need to continue to work together, and the agreement you reach needs to stand the test of time.

TIP

ANTICIPATE PROBLEMS

Look ahead, and try to see what problems might occur with the agreement. If you try to deal with a problem after it occurs, you will already be emotionally embroiled and may find it harder to deal with the issue objectively.

Asking insightful questions

A few careful questions before you leave the negotiation table could prevent emotional distress, frustration, and financial loss later. Reaching an agreement is only part of the negotiation. How that agreement will be managed and maintained is equally important. Disputes may arise, commitments may be missed, and circumstances may change, calling for renegotiation. You need to agree on a plan to address such issues. Ask some "what if" and "worst case scenario" questions, for example: "What circumstance would trigger a need to renegotiate?".

Planning for contingencies

After having identified potential problem areas in the agreement through insightful questioning, both parties should jointly prepare for any contingencies by designing plans and systems to address them. Both parties will then feel responsible for managing the agreement. Plans may include a mutually acceptable dispute resolution system, or perhaps a communication plan that allows for open discussions on a regular basis, or identifying potential triggers that would make renegotiation necessary. You may even better define roles, responsibilities, and deliverables, leaving less room for misunderstandings later.

Putting it in writing

People generally comply with written agreements more readily than verbal ones. Putting it in writing also clarifies the points of agreement and makes it harder for the other party to deny later. Once you have decided on contingency plans, put them in writing along with the primary agreement. Your agreement will now address not only what you agreed to, but also how it will be implemented and managed in the long term. Involve the other party in this and make sure you both feel comfortable, and that the language of the agreement accurately reflects your intent.

MANAGING THE AGREEMENT QUESTIONS

ISSUE	QUESTIONS
Miscommunication	• What kind of communication plan do we need to have in place to maintain this agreement? • What foreseeable gaps might occur in our communication? • What should be the frequency of our communication? • Which methods should we use for our communication?
Misunderstandings	• What misunderstandings could potentially occur around this agreement? • What can we do to decrease chances of these misunderstandings occuring? • What is our plan for dealing with these misunderstandings, if and when they do occur?
Missed deadlines and commitments	• What potential reasons may cause missed deadlines and commitments? • What can we do to decrease the chances of deadlines and commitments being missed? • What is our plan for dealing with missed deadlines and commitments when they do occur?
Breakdown in the agreement	• What potential situations might occur that would trigger the need for renegotiation? • Within how many days will we agree to communicate should such a situation become evident to one or both of us? • What is our plan for renegotiation should the need arise?

Saying "no"

Many of us avoid saying "no" even when we know we should. We are afraid of the defensiveness and anger it may cause, especially in a difficult person. But knowing how to say "no" constructively and positively is a skill we need in order to manage our relationships with authenticity and effectiveness.

Saying "no" constructively

Never agree to anything which is unacceptable to you just out of a fear of saying "no." John F. Kennedy's statement: "Don't fear to negotiate but don't negotiate out of fear" is a good rule to remember when working with difficult people. However, assertiveness heightens the potential for confrontation. To say "no" constructively, first explain your needs and constraints, invite them to suggest solutions, and conclude by telling them what you *can* do.

DON'T CONCEDE
If you feel uncomfortable saying yes, ask yourself why. If the reason is legitimate then resist the urge to say yes just to avoid an adverse reaction.

Replenishing the relationship

Even though the other party may comply with your constructive "no", the relationship could be affected. Also, in a long-term working relationship, there may be other times you need to say "no". You therefore have to balance your "no" with replenishing the relationship. Look for opportunities to nurture the relationship. Get together with the person for coffee or lunch and include them in events. Show them your "no" was not personal.

EXPLAIN YOUR CONSTRAINTS
Explain to the other person in a firm but friendly way what your constraints are and why you are unable to comply with their request.

LISTEN TO THEIR REQUEST

Make sure that the other person feels that their request has been heard, by summarizing and then checking your understanding with them.

Saying "no" constructively

TELL THEM WHAT YOU *ARE* WILLING TO DO

Let them know what you are willing to do for them which would not conflict with your needs or constraints.

BRAINSTORMING ALTERNATIVES

Invite them to jointly brainstorm alternative ways of satisfying their needs and requests.

REPLENISH THE RELATIONSHIP

Go out of your way to nurture the relationship and demonstrate that despite your declining their request, you still wish to be friends.

Making requests

When you want a difficult person to change their behavior, you will usually tell them what you *do not* want them to do. However, unless you request positive action that is specific, doable, and framed positively, their behavior is unlikely to change.

TIP

FRAME YOUR REQUEST BEFOREHAND

Always think about how to frame your request in advance. You will then be able to design a request that is more likely be well received and accepted.

Being specific

When making requests, be as specific as possible. Suppose you have a team member who you would like to participate more in team meetings. An ineffective way of communicating this would be to tell them that you would like them not to be so passive, or that you'd like them to participate more in meetings. An optimal request would be that you want at least two meaningful comments from them in every project meeting. By being specific and framing your request positively in terms of what you do want, you have communicated a clear directive that the other person can implement.

Making it doable

When you make a request, be sure that it is realistic, and that it does not conflict with the other party's needs, constraints, authority, or ability. Consider an example where you have decided to decrease the use of paper in your office, to contribute to the fight against global warming. Asking your staff to do everything electronically is not practical because there are times when hard copies may be absolutely necessary. A more suitable request would be to ask them to develop a policy for when to use electronic copies only. You have now made your request realistic and doable.

Requesting respectfully

Even difficult people need to feel respected. When that happens they tend to be a little less difficult, and when it does not, they will be even more difficult. When making a request, present it as a respectful request and not as a command, demand, or ultimatum. This will allow the other party to accept it without losing face. Let's say a co-worker habitually stops by your office to chat and interrupts your work. If you say: "Stop barging in here unannounced and wasting my time," it will make them feel disrespected, rejected, and defensive. Even if they cease their behavior they will not do so gladly and will continue to be difficult. A more respectful way would be to say: "I would love to chat more but I must complete these assignments. Would you like to continue after work?". The content is similar but the phraseology makes all the difference.

❓ ASK YOURSELF... ABOUT YOUR REQUEST

- Do I clearly understand what I need?
- Am I making a specific request?
- Is it framed positively (what I *do* want, and not what I *do not* want)?
- Is it doable from their perspective?
- Have I thought about how to phrase it so that it is respectful?

INTERPRETING PHRASEOLOGY

DISRESPECTFUL	RESPECTFUL
Do not interrupt me!	I would be happy to hear your thoughts once I have finished what I would like to say.
Do not be so angry!	Would you please talk to me about what is causing your anger?
You better get that done or else... !	Would you be willing to do that for us?
You are never around to help!	Could you be available on Monday afternoon to help with the office move?

Dealing with dishonesty

When confronted with dishonesty, you might feel betrayed, angry, anxious, or disappointed. You might be confused as to whether to confront it or ignore it, or how to confront it. There isn't a single answer for all situations, but there are guidelines you can apply to any given situation.

TIP

RESIST ACTING IMMEDIATELY
Take some time to consider whether the other person's actions were intentional. If they were, carefully decide what course of action to pursue.

Evaluating your options

When faced with dishonesty, do not immediately accuse the other person, as they will deny the allegation and become defensive. If you are not sure whether the other party is intentionally dishonest, or if the issue is unimportant, you may give them the benefit of the doubt. Where you find an established pattern of dishonesty and you need to continue the working relationship, you will need to address the dishonesty constructively. If a pattern of dishonesty appears, and the working relationship is not crucial, it may be time to disengage. When disengagement is not an option, consider taking the issue to higher management.

TIP

LET THE OTHER SAVE FACE
After confronting dishonesty, you could say something like: "I would like to hear more about your perspective, and discuss how we might overcome my feelings of uneasiness so that we can continue a successful working relationship."

Confronting dishonesty

If you have decided that confronting the dishonest person is the right course of action, provide specific instances of their deceitfulness, while at the same time allowing them to save face. For example, after telling them what led you to believe they were being dishonest, you could say: "I feel mislead at best and deceived at worst, and am uneasy about working with you further. What can you do that might overcome my anxiety?". This response confronts the dishonesty directly, even while allowing them to save face and negotiate a solution. Raising the issue explicitly will also discourage them from being dishonest with you in the future.

Disengaging
with dishonesty

If someone demonstrates a pattern of deliberate dishonesty, and your working relationship with them is not essential, you have the option of walking away. This option may also be appropriate if you have confronted them about their dishonesty with no effect. However, before disengaging, carefully weigh the costs, benefits, and practicality of terminating the working relationship. Once you decide to disengage it is a good idea to let them know what you intend to do and why. For example, after clearly explaining instances of how they deceived you, you might say: "Having felt misled and deceived on several occasions while working with you, I would feel more comfortable if we did not work together in the future. I hope you can respect my feelings." This lets them know in simple and unambiguous terms about where you stand with them.

Chapter 4

Managing the difficult person

Managing the difficult person can be a taxing and frustrating experience. The more techniques and skills you have in your repertoire, the better equipped you will be to work with them in a way that is fulfilling and rewarding for the both of you.

Starting with yourself

At times, when other people appear to be difficult, you will find that if you examine yourself it is you who is being difficult. They are merely reacting to your negative attitudes. Attitudes are contagious, so if you show leadership and set the right examples, these will help others behave appropriately.

TIP

USE COLORFUL POSTERS

Post colorful laminated posters of the desired attitudes and values you wish to reinforce around your department, so that your employees are constantly being reminded of them.

Setting an example

As a manager, you are the leader, and your example will be adopted by your group. If your employees are not working productively, perhaps they do not see you as a role model. If they are not accepting responsibility for their actions, be prepared to show more responsibility yourself. Acknowledge your mistakes, and you will notice their attitude improving. If your employees are not giving each other credit for good ideas and exceptional work, you should set an example and be generous with praise where it is deserved. Look at your employees to diagnose your own management attitude.

Seeking feedback

Your employees are a valuable source of feedback for improving your management attitude. You can find out how others perceive you, and create an environment where self-improvement is valued. When you ask for feedback, reassure them that constructive criticism is important and will not have negative consequences. Explain that you want to understand what it is like working for you. Ask them what they feel you do well, and where you could improve. Resist the urge to become defensive, and consider how you can use their feedback to improve your management attitude.

Being positive

There are some general positive attitudes that managers need to possess and demonstrate. A sense of humor is important: studies show that humor in the workplace promotes productivity and creativity. Remember not to take yourself too seriously. Do take an interest in the personal lives of your employees. Ask after the health of a spouse who was unwell or how their summer vacation was. Do not just give praise for a job well done, but also provide encouragement when your employees are finding things difficult. Being honest, transparent, and ethical are other positive traits.

TAKING RESPONSIBILITY

FAST TRACK	OFF TRACK
Understanding that your employees' behavior may be a reflection of yours	Being out of touch with your employees
Setting examples and being a role model for the way you want your employees to behave	Paying little attention to your employees' needs and concerns
Seeking feedback from your employees	Discouraging frequent, open, and honest communication
Taking an interest in their personal lives	Behaving in underhanded and unethical ways

Tackling difficult behavior

Your effectiveness as a manager is measured not only by how you manage your motivated people, but also by how you handle your difficult people. Awareness of common difficult behaviors and how to respond to them will give you the expertise to manage the less common ones too.

TIP

CHANNELLING BEHAVIOR

Manage others' difficult behavior by channelling it toward a productive resolution If you find yourself at a loss, ask them: "What would you do in my situation when faced with (describe their behavior)?".

Neutralizing the antagonist

The antagonist will always blame others for failures and seldom take responsibility for their own actions. To manage this behavior, redirect their attention back to themselves, and encourage them to take responsibility. Guide them in coming up with positive ideas, rather than getting drawn into their blame-game.

Defeating the defeatist

The defeatist is the perpetual pessimist in the group. Whenever an idea is presented, they throw up their arms and cry out that it will never work. This kills the idea even before it has been explored. In responding to the defeatist, ask them what specifically it is about the idea that they find unrealistic. This technique engages the defeatist constructively.

Interrupting the rambler

The rambler brings group productivity to a halt with their endless monologues. To regain control, use summarizing plus a closed-ended question. If the rambler is holding forth about some new product feature they are promoting, summarize their key points for them, then ask a closed-ended question. This interrupts their counter-productive behavior and gives you control.

Dealing with common difficult behaviors

THE ANTAGONIST Always blames others and does not take responsibility.

→

Redirect their attention back to themselves: ask them to suggest ways they can contribute positively to the project.

→

Example: "If you feel that the new person is not being supportive in the project, what could you do to improve that?".

THE DEFEATIST Cynical and pessimistic; believes no idea will ever work out.

→

Ask them what specifically they think will not work, and why. Ask them how the idea could be improved to make it work.

→

Example: "What exactly about the marketing plan is concerning you? What ideas could you suggest to improve it?".

THE RAMBLER Interrupts proceedings with endless, pointless monologs.

→

Interrupt them, and summarize their relevant points, then ask a closed-ended question to regain control.

→

Example: "Have you discussed this with marketing yet?" (closed-ended question). "Let's discuss that off-line."

TIP

MAKE IT SAFE WHEN ASKING QUESTIONS

When questioning employees about job satisfaction and challenges, explain that you want them to perform better—not dismiss them—and only honesty and openness will facilitate this.

Aligning tasks with competencies

If an employee is given a job for which they are not trained or which they do not find satisfying, it can cause loss of motivation and difficult behavior. If a highly creative person is put into the accounting department to crunch numbers, they will be unmotivated and will underperform. When you notice an unmotivated employee, try to find out how they feel about their job. Ask questions such as: "What do you particularly enjoy about your job?", and "What do you find most challenging?". Another useful question to ask is: "If you could describe your ideal job, what might that look like?". These questions will give you a sense of whether their tasks are aligned with their skills. If not, you will either need to give them training in the skills that they are lacking, or perhaps move them to a position that is more aligned with their abilities. Before you can determine the alignment between tasks and competencies, however, be sure that the task and its desired results have been clearly defined and that the employee understands exactly what is required of them. Otherwise, the problem could just be a lack of clear understanding instead of a loss of necessary skills.

CASE STUDY

Fitting competencies to roles

A manufacturing company adopted a new pay-for-performance scheme which would be benchmarked by standards of efficiency. One particular employee was resistant to this because her strength was quality. Realizing that her ability to work to high standards was no longer aligned with the company's new focus on efficiency made her feel dejected. Her manager realized the problem and did not wish to lose a valuable and hard-working employee. He created a new position in which she was to oversee quality so as to ensure that it would not be compromised in the name of efficiency. By making sure that her tasks were aligned with her competencies, he was able to retain a satisfied and motivated employee who would advance the interests of the company significantly.

Meeting employees' needs

Besides obvious needs such as a suitable work environment, safety, and respect, employees are motivated by a sense of being valued. They should feel recognized for good work. Find things you can acknowledge them for, even if it is something small. Responsibility is another way of motivating people. Look for opportunities to give your employees responsibility in line with their capability. Suppose in a meeting on increasing sales someone suggests the development of a new distribution channel. You could say: "That sounds interesting. Could you research feasibility using our SWOT analysis method and suggest an implementation plan at the next meeting?". Giving them a specific task and added responsibility will motivate them.

RECOGNIZE SINCERELY

Any contrived acknowledgement on your part will be transparent to employees and will not motivate.

Using incentives and rewards

An incentive-and-reward program is a good way to keep your employees motivated and performing well. Airlines do this with their customers through frequent-flier rewards and large retailers encourage buyers with special discount coupons. A similar system can be used to drive your employees' performance. An incentive-and-reward program can include paid time off, trips, profit sharing, free merchandise, and employee-of-the-month contests with associated perks. Involve your employees in designing such a program. Also consult with HR, accounting, and legal on the plan. Make sure the plan is clearly communicated and well understood.

Analyzing performance

The process of reviewing performance and setting goals often generates anxiousness among managers regarding their employees' reactions. This robs them of the opportunities that performance reviews and goal-setting offer to improve team management. Knowing how to conduct reviews and set objectives is essential in leading the difficult person.

Understanding the purpose

The term "performance review" is slightly misleading, as it implies an emphasis on past performance. The purpose of such as review is to set objectives for the future: to analyze the employee's strengths and weaknesses and provide constructive feedback. It should be positive and objective at all times. When the employee leaves the review, they should feel like a valuable member of the team with the skill to contribute positively. See yourself as a mentor and not as a judge.

Involving the employee

A performance review should be collaborative. Engage the employee so that they participate and feel involved in the process. As points of departure for further discussion, ask them about their accomplishments over the past year, and what they want to change about their job. When giving feedback, avoid vagueness and ambiguity. Be specific and provide detailed observations that illustrate the issue at hand. This will let your employee know exactly what they need to do to improve.

Setting achievable goals for your employees

COLLABORATIVE
Make sure you involve your employees in goal setting by seeking their input, ideas, and suggestions. Aim for mutual agreement.

MANAGEABLE
Articulate goals in specific and realistic terms. "Reducing time to market from 12 to nine weeks" is more helpful than "Reducing time to market."

MEASURABLE
Establish agreed-upon benchmarks to measure whether goals have been met. Document goals and benchmarks and share the results with employees.

TIME-BOUND
Jointly determine timeframes within which results can realistically be expected. Definitive timeframes create a sense of urgency.

MONITORED
Set up regular communication for monitoring and feedback. This will ensure employees stay on course, and allow for mid-course corrections.

Spotting the symptoms

When an employee is performing poorly, look for symptoms of demotivation such as lethargy, lack of enthusiasm, lateness, frequent health problems, anger, depression, or any other sign that all is not well. If such symptoms are present, view their poor performance as a call for help rather than as incompetence or a refusal to cooperate. Look for what might be causing their demotivation and how you can help. Consider causes such as objectives not being clearly defined, insufficient feedback, tasks being too challenging, or a lack of confidence in their own ability. There could also be personal reasons, such as an ailing parent or marital problems. Make sure you try to uncover any underlying problem that may be present.

Talking about poor performance

Once you have identified poor performance and spotted behavior patterns that suggest an underlying problem, you need to address the problem with the employee. Talk to them in a supportive way and try to jointly figure out what the problem is. You might say: "Your performance of late has been below par. Last week you were not ready with the presentation. The previous week, accounting found several mistakes in your financial report. I have also noticed a general lack of enthusiasm in you and am concerned. I think you are going through a difficult time, and I would like to help you." With this approach you have sent a message of understanding, sympathy, and support, allowing your employee to explain the situation to you.

TIP

ASK YOUR EMPLOYEES FOR INPUT

Always try to elicit input from your employees when resolving problems. People do not like to have solutions imposed upon them.

Knowing your limitations

There will be times when, after listening, careful questioning, suggesting ideas, and engaging the employee in designing possible solutions, you still fail to resolve their behavior. This is the time to recognize your limitations and seek help elsewhere. Do not see this as a failure on your part. Just as a doctor sometimes needs to refer a patient to a specialist, you might at times need to refer an employee to someone who has more expertise or experience in handling the issue. Use all the resources available to you. Get advice from other managers. Get help from executives. Speak to the appropriate people at HR and where necessary get help through your company's employee assistance program. Don't try to solve a problem that is beyond your competency and expertise. Accept that you can help others realize their potential, but that you cannot change others or mould them in your own image. Even if you feel that you have been unsuccessful, use the opportunity to improve your skills by asking yourself what lessons you can learn from the experience.

TIP

DISCUSS YOUR IDEAS

Talk to your mangers, colleagues, and mentors about how best to tackle the difficult employee. Besides helping you with the problem, it will also expand your learning experience.

✔ CHECKLIST EXAMINING POOR PERFORMANCE:

	YES	NO
• Does the employee have a clear understanding of their goals and are they realistic?	☐	☐
• Are they receiving adequate and timely feedback?	☐	☐
• Do they have the ability, training, and resources to perform the required tasks?	☐	☐
• Are they bored with too little challenge, or overwhelmed with too much challenge?	☐	☐
• Are there personal issues that they are dealing with?	☐	☐

Coaching your employee

Coaching* is a useful, though under-utilized, means to drive your employee to higher levels of self-awareness, discovery, action, and productivity. As a manager, it is important that you have the coaching skills to draw out the best from your employees, even diffficult ones, for their benefit and for the benefit of your organization.

*Coaching —
Engaging the employee in a thought-provoking, creative process that inspires them to maximize their personal and professional potential.

Understanding coaching

Coaching is a process that pushes your employee into recognizing professional obstacles, creatively devising action plans to overcome those obstacles, and evaluating the results. It is not the coach who develops the solutions but the employee. The coach is the facilitator who inspires the employee to go ahead and fix the problems. The coaching objective is to help your employee gain greater clarity, new insights and perspectives, organized thoughts, and the ability to arrive at their own solutions.

TIP

GIVE THE EMPLOYEE TIME

When you are coaching and have asked a question, wait patiently and quietly for the employee to answer. Don't try to avoid the discomfort of silence by offering your own answer.

Questioning

The management guru Peter Drucker once said of leadership: "The leader of the past knew how to tell; the leader of the future will know how to ask". Asking questions that lead to deep thinking is the coach's most important skill. Not all questions generate deep thinking. The question "What is on your to-do list today?" does not inspire thought. The revision: "Which three tasks on your list will have the greatest impact?" will force the employee to think. When coaching, look for questions that inspire deeper thought and unlock new ideas. It is those questions from which your employee will learn and benefit the most.

Balancing encouragement

When your employee is working hard in a coaching session, give encouragement as far as posssible. For example: "I really appreciated your rigorous self-analysis and am impressed by the insight it produced." This recognizes their effort and motivates them further. Make sure your encouragement is genuine. Balance encouragement measure-for-measure with challenge. Be aware that challenges need to stretch your employee beyond their current thinking and actions, but not so far that it goes beyond their abilities. You will need to assess this based on your knowledge of your employee.

TIP

USE BODY LANGUAGE EFFECTIVELY

When interacting with the employee, make sure to maintain eye contact and lean in toward them. This will indicate genuine interest, attention, honesty, and trust on your part.

COACHING: THE FOUR PHASES

PHASE	USEFUL QUESTIONS TO ASK
Identifying Helping the employee identify the core issue that needs to be addressed. If there are multiple issues, use this phase to break down the issues into manageable tasks.	• Where are you stuck? • What is the most important thing you need to do today? • What topics would give you the greatest return for this investment of time?
Discovering Helping the employee discover their needs, wants, options, resources, assets —anything that could make an immediate difference to their performance.	• What are your initial thoughts in approaching this problem? • What have you already tried? And what were the results? • What are some options to deal with this?
Planning for action Helping the employee design a specific action plan that is realistic and practical. This plan is driven by the information gathered in the discovering phase.	• What action do you plan to take? By when? • Of all the options we listed in the discovery phase, which would be the best action? • What resources do you need to implement this plan? • How could you mitigate the risks?
Evaluating Helping the employee put systems into place to measure the success of their action plan.	• What systems do you need to put into place to hold yourself accountable? • What criteria will you use to measure your success?

Dealing with difficult teams

As a manager, you may find yourself challenged not just by difficult persons, but also by difficult and uncooperative teams. Being able to resolve issues between teams is a critical managerial skill. It involves creating the right conditions for dialog, developing collaboration, and maintaining relationships.

TIP

ESTABLISH ROLES AND RULES

When facilitating dialog, establish roles and agree on ground rules. Roles might include someone to chair the discussion. An example of a ground rule could be only one person speaking at a time. This will keep the discussion productive.

Facilitating dialog

Consider two competing teams in your organization. Each team is certain that it is working on a product that will boost revenue. Each fights for budgets, resources, and visibility, believing that their product deserves priority. This conflict results in reduced productivity, missed deadlines, increased costs, inefficient use of resources, and eroded morale. In this situation, your first step is to facilitate dialog between the teams. You need a rigorous appraisal of each team's goals, objectives, needs, and concerns. Make each team feel heard and understood, and a collaborative atmosphere will soon develop.

Working toward collaboration

Once you have an understanding of the needs and concerns of each team, look for creative ways to meet those needs. In a case of competing product development teams, for example, you may find ways of integrating products that will add value, or perhaps ways of collaborating on some specific component common to both products, or even a joint marketing campaign. Seeking creative ways of aligning teams' objectives can turn potential conflict into collaboration.

TIP

GENERATE A RANGE OF IDEAS

When brainstorming for ideas that could satisfy the needs of both teams, generate a range of ideas before evaluating and deciding. This will broaden your range of options.

Going forward

Even after a working relationship has been developed between the two teams, effort is still needed to maintain and manage the relationship going forward. It is useful to document the agreement reached between the teams in a memorandum of understanding. This helps build compliance and pre-empts misunderstandings. Open communication between the teams should be encouraged, as problems usually arise when effective communication is absent.

CASE STUDY

Using feedback

An American company used customer feedback to improve its products. The marketing department contacted customers to obtain feedback, which they passed on to product development. Product development was to act on the information and produce new and improved products. Marketing accused product development of not fulfilling the company's promise to use customer feedback to improve products. Product development accused marketing of not appreciating the resources and manpower required to design and develop the new products that customers suggested. Tensions between the two teams grew. Then both teams worked toward collaboration. They created a joint work group with representatives from both marketing and product development, which would interface with customers and mediate issues between marketing and product development. The company's products improved as a result.

Including the difficult person

A team is greater than the sum of its members. When faced with a difficult team member, you may be tempted to insulate yourself from them. However, including them as a valued member of the team will help alleviate their difficult behavior. Frequent interaction, encouragement, and delegation are effective ways of including the difficult employee.

Interacting frequently

LET EMPLOYEES DEVISE THEIR OWN SOLUTIONS
When delegating, give your employees space to find their own solutions. By trying to impose your own thinking, you will defeat the purpose of delegation.

Frequent personal interaction with employees makes them feel connected to you and the team. A few moments of talking to an employee will promote satisfaction in them about the work they are doing. Greeting them by name adds meaningfulness to the interaction. Show an interest in their personal lives, their outside interests. This will build the relationship and provide you with information. Ask work-related questions, too. They will feel they are valued by you and the organization. A sense of worth and importance is necessary for people to perform at their best.

Providing encouragement

BE GENUINE
When offering encouragement, be genuine, authentic, and sincere at all times. Lacking sincerity, patronizing, and pretending will be transparent and will backfire on you.

To make people feel they are valued team members acknowledge jobs well done and give encouragement for challenges not yet met. This does not mean that constructive criticism is not important, but it will be better received if it is balanced with acknowledgment and encouragement where appropriate. Bear in mind that you can find words of praise even with difficult people. When offering encouragement, be specific. For example: "I really appreciated your innovative approach in helping the customer" is better than "Great job!". It shows you know what was involved, and helps your praise seem authentic.

Delegating

A good way to demonstrate belief and trust in an employee, and make them feel valued and included, is to delegate tasks and responsibilities to them. Besides showing your team that you trust and respect the person, this will also demonstrate that you are helping the person grow professionally. That person in turn will trust and respect you. Do not just delegate to your best workers, as this will breed resentment among others. Make sure to include everyone according to their capability, including the difficult employee. They may surprise you by how well they rise to the challenge. When delegating, start with smaller tasks and allow your employees' confidence to build before assigning larger projects. An employee who feels you trust them will reciprocate with a desire to please, and even the difficult person may make an effort at being reasonable.

HOW TO... DELEGATE

Communication: Explain accurately what it is you need done, by whom and by when, and the expected results.

Context: Explain how the task links to the overall project and who is in charge of the other components of the project.

Standards: Set realistic and achievable standards to measure the success of the task.

Authority: Assign to your employee the authority that is required to get the task done.

Support: Provide resources, funding, training, and access to the employee as needed for the task.

Commitment: Make sure the employee knows the task to be accomplished, and that you have answered their questions.

 IN FOCUS... CONSTRUCTIVE CRITICISM

People can be resistant to criticism, even the constructive kind. They become more resistant when the only time their manager communicates with them is to provide negative feedback. Ongoing interaction with an employee will allow criticism to be better received. A manager who interacts with an employee frequently can congratulate them on a successful project and also provide constructive criticism. Because of the regular communication between them, this will be received positively.

Implementing the last resort

When all your efforts at resolving an employee's attitude and performance are fruitless, it shows that there are irreconcilable differences between them and the organization. The only remaining option then might be termination of their employment. Knowing how to communicate this, and how to tackle its emotional and legal aspects, helps minimize associated damage.

*Dissmissal —
To terminate employment due to unacceptable levels of performance or behavior.

Being familiar with legalities

A carelessly handled dismissal* can lead to a costly wrongful-termination or discrimination lawsuit. It is therefore important you are familiar with company procedures and legal requirements with regard to terminating an employee. Consult HR for specific policies and procedures. These will often include: how to document poor performance or problematic behavior, necessary steps for the termination process, and potential union issues. Be vigilant in following these procedures and consult with your legal counsel.

Communicating the bad news

When communicating the dismissal, look to preserve the employee's dignity and respect. Deliver the bad news in private to avoid humiliating the person. When dismissing them, speak in objective, non-judgmental terms. For example: "The improvement standards we both agreed on last quarter have not been met. We have made a decision to dismiss you." as opposed to: "You disappointed us by not meeting the standards we agreed upon—you're fired." If you are feeling anger toward the employee, postpone this discussion until you have calmed down. Show them sympathy, and give them an opportunity to vent any resentment they may feel toward you or the organization.

Helping employee transition

A disgruntled employee who talks about how badly they were treated can give your organization a poor reputation and make it hard for you to hire in the future. They might also talk to other employees and erode morale. Help the fired employee with the transition to another organization so that they feel well treated and are less likely to spread negative reports. Allow them, where possible, time to use the office to look for a new job. If HR offers career counseling services, help your employee access them. Offer to provide references, and try to arrange the best possible severance package. Showing compassion and goodwill will help soften the blow, and preserve your organization's integrity.

TIP

ASK HUMAN RESOURCES TO BE PRESENT

HR can help answer questions, serve as a witness to the discussion, and be a neutral voice in assisting with any adverse emotional or physical reactions.

DECIDING WHEN TO TERMINATE

DISMISS IMMEDIATELY	WARN AND PROCEED WITH DOCUMENTATION	NO CAUSE TO DISMISS
Carrying a weapon to work.	Persistently underperforming.	Taking a day off work that was legitimate under law or civic duty.
Revealing trade secrets.	Abusing sick leave or any privilege.	Blowing the whistle on something illegal.
Being blatantly dishonest.	Being consistently tardy or absent.	Filing for worker's compensation.
Endangering co-workers.	Being insubordinate.	Reporting health and safety code violations.
Being involved in sexual harassment.	Having a destructive attitude and being a negative influence.	Electing to belong or not to belong to a union.
Engaging in criminal activity, including involvement with illegal drugs.	Refusing to follow instructions.	Being a particular race, gender, age, sexual orientation, or marital status, or being pregnant.

Index

Acknowledgments

Author's acknowledgments

Working with the DK team as they breathed creative energy into my manuscript has been a privilege. Many thanks to all who worked so diligently. To Daniel Mills who managed the project and provided invaluable input, to Ankush Saikia who led his team magnificently and guided me tirelessly, and to Arunesh Talapatra, our talented designer. Also to Peter Jones who recognized my ability. With the encouragement of my wife, Chanah, and my nine children, the journey was as satisfying as the destination.

Publisher's acknowledgments

The publisher would like to thank Margaret Parrish and Charles Wills for coordinating Americanization.

Picture credits

The publisher would like to thank the following for their kind permission to reproduce their photographs:

Corbis: W. Perry Conway 4-5; Image Source 60; Matthias Kulka 12-13; Frans Lanting 42-43; Joseph Sohm 58-59; Getty Images: BLOOMimage 11; Gary S. Chapman 26-27; Matthias Clamer 40; Jeffrey Coolidge 24-25; DAJ 68; George Diebold 55; Macduff Everton 1; Shannon Fagan 46-47; Image Source 68; UpperCut Images 36; Ryan McVay 38-39; Buero Monaco 51; Gregor Schuster 30; Luca Trovato 28-29; Jeppe Wikstrom 64; iStockphoto.com: Kun Jiang 11; Jeff Metzger 19, 20; Alexander Vasilyev 57

Jacket images: Front: Alamy Images: Mira

All other images © Dorling Kindersley
For further information see:
www.dkimages.com